Gifted and Talented Workbook
Seventh Grade

Stereotypes: *Native Americans*

There is a common stereotype of the Native A...
headdress with eagle feathers, and having a red...
depiction? Share your thoughts below:

Google

"Seven Habits of Highly Critical Thinkers"

Use a computer, tablet or phone to use Google to find the article by T...
Critical Thinkers" and answer these questions:

1st What is critical thinking?

2nd What is truth?

3rd What is a habit?

What are the seven habits listed by...

1
2
3
4
5
6
7

Fun with License Plates

DNTSTME   I MT BYK (COLORADO)   Z2KWET

(WASHINGTON) LIL WMP   ON AXDNT   PULLLEZ

Secret Messages

1 _____   2 _____   3 _____
4 _____   5 _____   6 _____

Which license plate was the **easiest**? _____
Which license plate was the **hardest**? _____

Which license plate is the **funniest**? _____
Make up two new license plates with a secret message

New Plate   Secret Message

California _____

NEW YORK _____

120 Thinking Activities

C. Mahoney

Life is about choices...

A to Z Word Puzzle

Use all 26 letters from A to Z to complete the words in this puzzle.

A B C D E F G H I J K L M N O P Q R S T U V W X Y Z

Fun with License Plates

Secret Messages

| 1 _____ | 2 _____ | 3 _____ |
| 4 _____ | 5 _____ | 6 _____ |

Which license plate was the **easiest**? _____

Which license plate was the **hardest**?

_____

Which license plate is the **funniest**? _____

Make up two new license plates with a secret message

New Plate   **Secret Message**

= _____

= _____

Analyze and Describe

List eight interesting things that you see on the back of this quarter.

 1   5

2   6

3   7

4   8

Fingerspelling Alphabet

Hidden Nouns: *Summer*

Find the hidden words in these boxes (just like Boggle). Each letter in a
word must touch the next (horizontally, vertically, or diagonally).

G	Y	A	P
R	O	S	L
N	U	A	H
S	D	E	W

	Z	I	X	
B	S	M	T	J
P	O	S	S	V
W	I	B	L	E
	N	P	R	

A	O	O	B
T	C	K	G
I	A	R	A
V	O	N	P

I	V	O	G
E	A	M	A
R	T	C	E
A	E	H	B

L	E	A	L
O	C	N	L
Y	O	K	A
T	P	E	B

Summer nouns

⬇

Other words you found

⬇

Divergent Thinking...

What do men and women do with the **hair** on their head and face?

Directions: Answer this question with as many answers as you can think of.

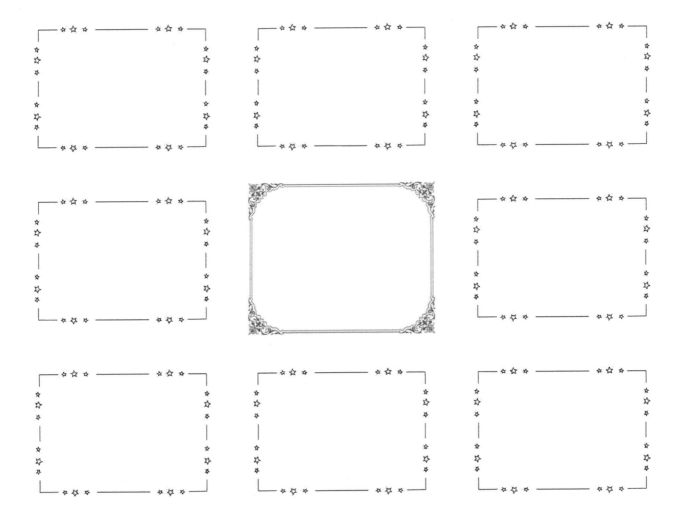

What Causes Blindness?

Use a <u>computer</u>, <u>tablet</u> or <u>phone</u> to search online for information about the causes of blindness. Start at YouTube and search for "what causes blindness" and share your observations below:

①

②

③

④

ONLINE SOURCES OF INFORMATION:

ANNOYING BUGS

Here is a collection of the most annoying bugs ever, the ones that give people the creeps, the itchies, the "Squash that thing right now!" cries for help. They can be **horizontal**, **vertical**, **diagonal**, **forwards**, or **backwards**. Can you find them?

A	N	T	A	N	T	A	N	T	A	N	T	A	N	T	A
C	O	C	K	R	O	A	C	H	B	V	A	V	S	X	N
T	E	J	A	H	K	N	G	U	B	K	N	I	T	S	T
N	C	N	N	G	M	L	R	E	W	Q	T	Q	T	A	A
A	D	F	T	N	A	T	A	N	T	A	J	N	N	K	N
N	H	N	G	I	Y	L	F	E	S	R	O	H	A	L	T
T	A	L	F	G	P	A	N	T	P	T	V	O	B	M	A
J	K	T	N	A	Y	E	U	I	I	N	S	R	N	E	N
L	O	U	S	E	N	P	D	O	D	A	T	N	A	D	T
T	T	N	A	F	M	L	C	E	E	D	N	E	N	E	H
N	I	I	F	T	N	A	V	Q	R	W	F	T	T	P	T
A	U	T	Y	L	F	E	S	U	O	H	E	R	Y	I	F
N	Q	N	D	T	B	V	X	A	A	I	O	T	U	L	A
T	S	A	S	N	W	T	N	Z	S	K	P	N	E	L	N
T	O	U	W	A	N	T	N	A	D	C	L	A	K	I	T
N	M	Y	S	A	N	T	E	A	F	I	G	H	J	M	N
A	T	P	R	G	U	B	D	E	B	T	N	A	T	N	A

Find these words: cockroach, centipede, millipede, wasp, hornet, housefly, horsefly, mosquito, flea, louse, tick, stinkbug, bedbug, spider, ant

Bonus: How many ANTS can you find in this puzzle? There are lots of them, so look carefully. ____

Stereotypes: *Native Americans*

There is a common stereotype of the Native American wearing a feathered headdress with eagle feathers, and having a red face. What is wrong with this depiction? Share your thoughts below:

_____

_____

_____

_____

_____

_____

_____

_____

_____

_____

_____

_____

_____

St. Patrick's Day: *Persons*

Identify these St. Patrick's Day words using your fingerspelling chart.

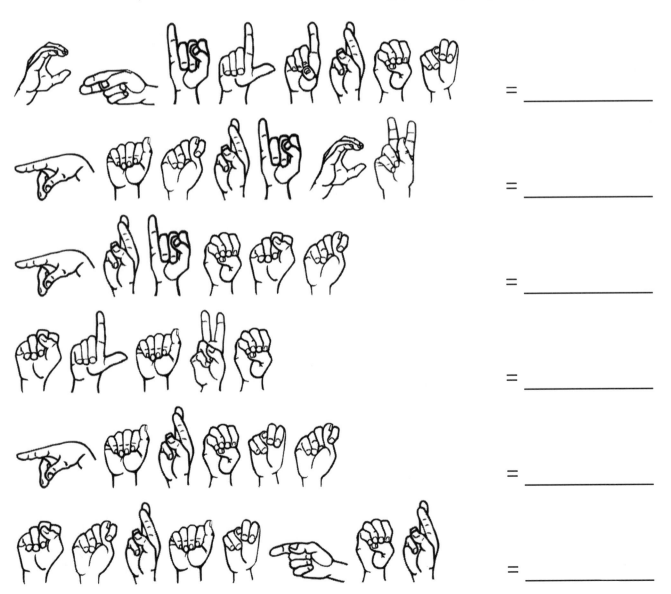

= _____

= _____

= _____

= _____

= _____

= _____

What is wrong with stealing?

In the movie "Black Panther," stealing things leads to anger and violence. Use a <u>computer</u>, <u>tablet</u> or <u>phone</u> to see what others have said online about stealing.

1

2

3

4

5

Possible consequences for stealing:

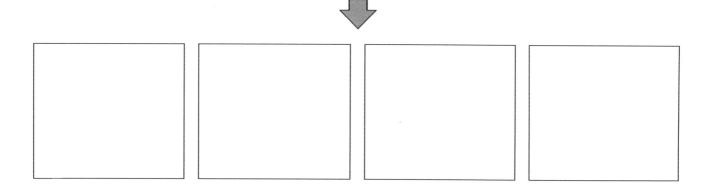

Multiplication: What Is Missing?

×	1	2	3	4	5	6	7	8	9	10
1	1				5	6			9	10
2			6	8	10			16	18	
3	3	6		12			21	24	27	
4		8	12	16	20	24		32	36	40
5	5	10		20		30			45	
6	6		18	24			42		54	60
7			21		35	42	49	56	63	
8	8	16	24		40	48		64	72	80
9			27	36		54	63	72	81	90
10	10			40	50	60	70		90	100

Thinking questions...

1 What is the largest odd two-digit missing number? _____
2 What is the smallest even two-digit missing number? _____
3 Which multiples of six were missing? _____, _____, _____, _____
4 Which even numbers were missing? _____, _____, _____, _____, _____, _____, _____, _____, _____, _____, _____, _____, _____, _____, _____, _____

How to make people laugh...

Describe six things that you must do with your legs and arms and head and fingers and toes and mouth in order to <u>make people laugh</u>.

First	Second

Third	Fourth

Fifth	Sixth

Wakanda vs America

Use a <u>computer</u>, <u>tablet</u> or <u>phone</u> to learn about the imaginary Kingdom of Wakanda from the movie "Black Panther." Compare it to the United States of America, and explain ways in which they are similar and different:

_____

_____

_____

_____

_____

_____

_____

_____

_____

_____

_____

_____

_____

_____

_____

_____

_____

_____

_____

Developing Character

Writing prompt: What makes you angry? What discriminatory actions of others causes you to turn from a <u>happy</u> and <u>talkative</u> person into an <u>angry</u> and <u>explosive</u> person?

_____

_____

_____

_____

_____

_____

_____

_____

_____

_____

_____

_____

_____

_____

_____

                         _____

                         _____

                         _____

                         _____

                         _____

                         _____

Developing Character

Writing prompt: Who has <u>helped</u> you recently, reaching out a hand or offering you something they had, even though they didn't need to, just to be nice?

_____

_____

_____

_____

_____

_____

_____

_____

_____

_____

_____

_____

_____

_____

_____

_____

_____

_____

_____

YOU DON'T NEED A REASON TO HELP PEOPLE.

HOW TO MAKE A DECISION...

What are some important <u>decisions</u> that you made? No one decided
for you. You decided. You chose. You picked. List eight of them below.

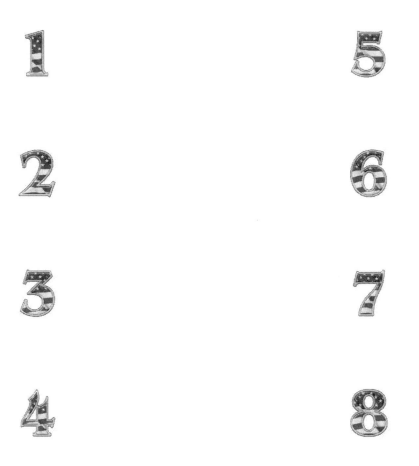

1

2

3

4

5

6

7

8

Veterans Day: *Persons*

Identify these Veterans Day words using your finger-spelling chart.

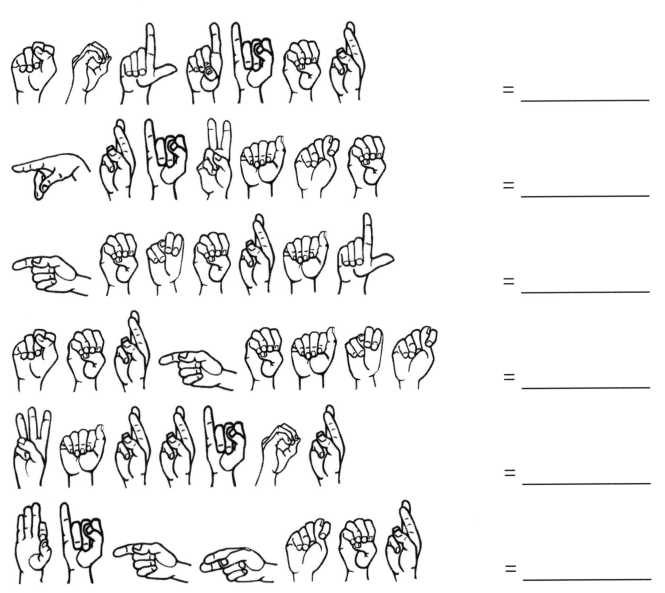

= _____

= _____

= _____

= _____

= _____

= _____

How to take a selfie...

Describe six moments when it is okay to take a <u>selfie</u> with someone else.

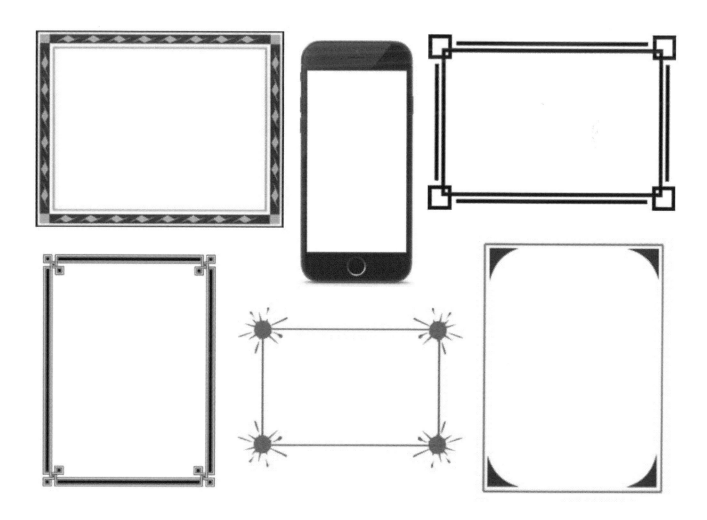

What is the purpose of school?

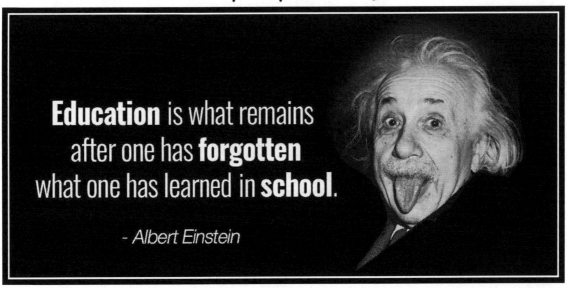

Education is what remains after one has **forgotten** what one has learned in **school**.

- Albert Einstein

Why is it good for you to go to school? Give five reasons:

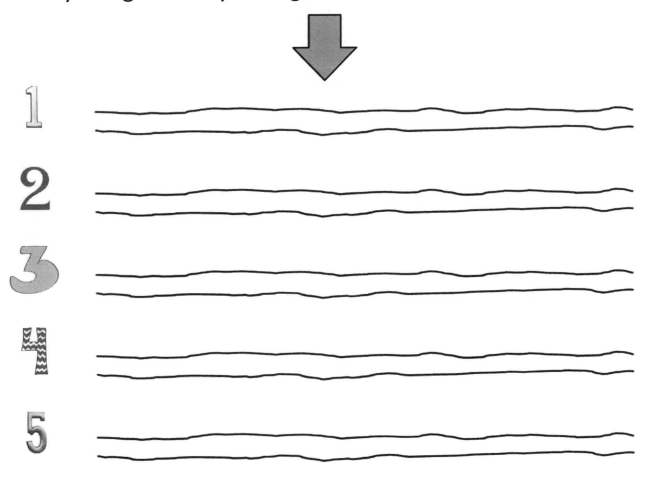

1

2

3

4

5

What questions do you think about?

"The only source of knowledge is experience."

"Learn from yesterday. Live for today. Hope for tomorrow. The important thing is to not stop questioning."

What questions about life and the universe do you have?

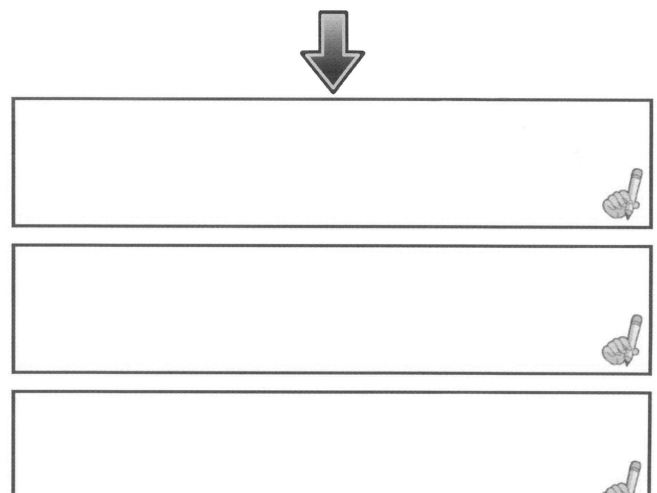

"Seven Habits of Highly Critical Thinkers"

Use a <u>computer</u>, <u>tablet</u> or <u>phone</u> to use Google to find the article by Tim van Gelder entitled "Seven Habits of Highly Critical Thinkers" and answer these questions:

1st What is **critical thinking**?

2nd What is **truth**?

3rd What is a **habit**?

What are the seven habits listed by Tim van Gelder?

1

2

3

4

5

6

7

(https://wspucla.wordpress.com/2013/02/25/monday-money-how-to-critically-engage-with-a-text/)

What do you literally see in this cartoon?

What is this cartoon trying to tell you?

Decoding California

Analyze each California image and decode its secrets. What do the letters and images represent? They are there for a reason. Figure it out and write what you notice.

What <u>letters</u> or <u>words</u> do you see?

What <u>things</u> or <u>objects</u> do you see?

What **business** or **organization** is this symbol for?

What <u>letters</u> or <u>words</u> do you see?

What <u>things</u> or <u>objects</u> do you see?

What **business** or **organization** is this symbol for?

What <u>letters</u> or <u>words</u> do you see?

What <u>things</u> or <u>objects</u> do you see?

What **business** or **organization** is this symbol for?

Decoding California

Analyze each California image and decode its secrets. What do the letters and images represent? They are there for a reason. Figure it out and write what you notice.

What <u>letters</u> or <u>words</u> do you see?	What <u>letters</u> or <u>words</u> do you see?	What <u>letters</u> or <u>words</u> do you see?
What <u>things</u> or <u>objects</u> do you see?	What <u>things</u> or <u>objects</u> do you see?	What <u>things</u> or <u>objects</u> do you see?
What **business** or **organization** is this symbol for?	What **business** or **organization** is this symbol for?	What **business** or **organization** is this symbol for?

Geometric Activities

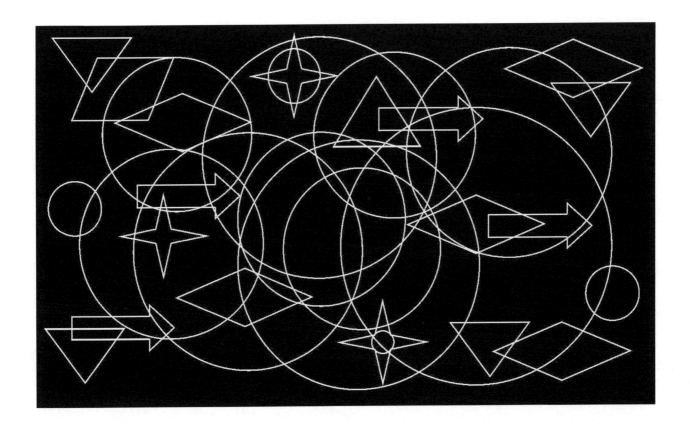

How many circles?

A) Twelve circles
B) Thirteen circles
C) Fourteen circles
D) Fifteen circles
E) Sixteen circles

What is the hidden message on each license plate?

_____   _____

Geometric Activities

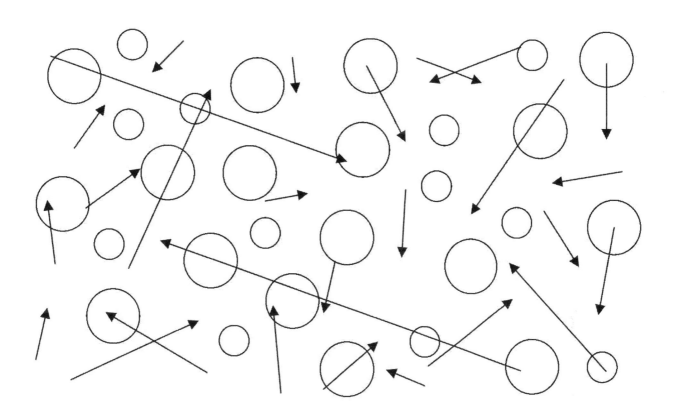

How many circles?

A) Twenty-six circles
B) Twenty-seven circles
C) Twenty-eight circles
D) Twenty-nine circles
E) Thirty circles

What is the hidden message on each license plate?

_____   _____

Adjectives and Nouns: Bats

Match the ADJECTIVE on the left to the NOUN on the right. Use arrows.

juicy	cave
thin	echoes
beady	pups
nervous	fruit
escaping	colony
dark	eyes
annoying	bat
high-pitched	wings
gray	sounds
crowded	insects

Use several of these phrases in five sentences below:

1 _____

2 _____

3 _____

4 _____

5 _____

Adjectives and Nouns: Buffalos

Match the ADJECTIVE on the left to the NOUN on the right. Use arrows.

stampeding	mountains
soft	horns
enormous	buffalo
delicious	flies
sharp	fields
wiggling	hooves
stamping	shoulders
distant	grass
buzzing	calves
curious	tail

Use several of these phrases in five sentences below:

1 _____

2 _____

3 _____

4 _____

5 _____

What do you notice about this stamp?

List six things you notice about the <u>words</u>, <u>numbers</u> and <u>pictures</u> on this stamp.

1

2

3

4

A Postage Stamp *about* **Airplanes**

Search online for an **interesting airplane postage stamp**. Use colored pencils, crayons or markers as you draw this stamp. Be neat and accurate.

Do you ever wonder why?

 Why do snakes stay on the ground?

 Why do snakes slither away?

 Why do snakes eat other animals?

 Why do snakes stick out their tongue?

Do you ever wonder why?

1 Why do trees fall down?

2 Why does a forest smell weird?

3 Why do people chop down trees?

4 Why do animals live in trees?

Divergent Thinking...

What <u>healthy</u> <u>food</u> might the President eat for breakfast?

Directions: Answer this question with as many answers as you can think of.

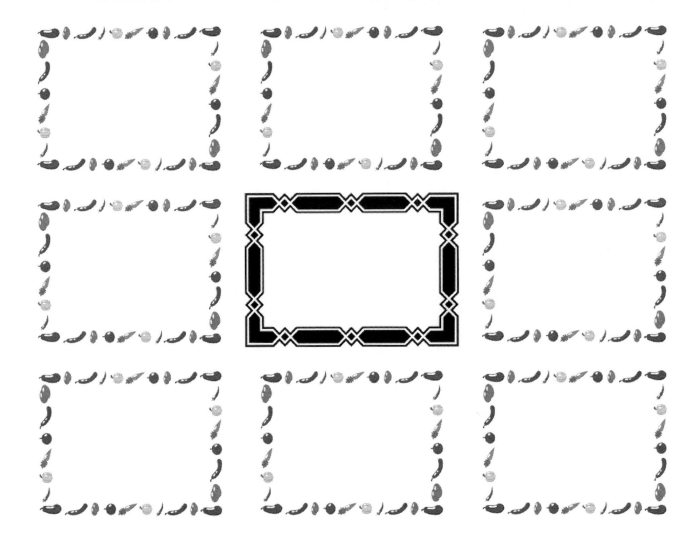

Hidden Nouns: *Space*

Find the hidden words in these boxes (just like Boggle). Each letter in a word must touch the next (horizontally, vertically, or diagonally).

R	O	I	D
E	L	K	M
T	S	L	Y
E	N	A	P

	Z	I	X	
B	S	M	T	J
P	O	S	S	V
W	I	B	L	E
	N	P	R	

Y	T	I	N
C	A	O	B
W	O	A	R
M	E	T	S

U	U	R	E
Y	S	C	M
R	A	M	Y
G	L	A	X

U	H	T	A
S	N	E	R
R	B	E	S
U	V	I	V

Space nouns 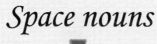	Other words you found
How many SPACE NOUNS did you find? **11-14** Good job. **15** = You rock!!!	How many other words did you find? **15-19** Good job. **20** = You rock!!!

Insect Unscramble

spshoprager

benoheye

treftluby

bdyaulg

emertit

onlygradf

uiqotamo

telebe

lipreactarl

kecitrc

_____

_____

_____

_____

_____

_____

_____

_____

_____

_____

The dragonfly and the very fast mosquito

a mosquito that just noticed the predator

four transparent wings

the SUN SHINING dOWN ON THE eaRTH

two enormous compound eyes

a grasper on the end of its tail

a spider lurking silently in her web

ants crawling on the plant

a lizard lurking down below

six strong legs to hold onto a leaf or prey

A TREE FULL OF YOUNG SONGBIRDS MAKING LOTS OF NOISE

_____

_____

_____

_____

_____

_____

_____

_____

_____

Did you know...

1 Dragonflies of long ago (300,000,000 years ago) had two-foot _____ spans.

2 A dragonfly can _____ 36 m.p.h..

3 A dragonfly has a _____ spot so hawks swoop from the rear to capture and eat them.

4 The dragonfly is the _____ insect on earth.

5 There are over 4,800 _____ of dragonflies.

6 A dragonfly rests with its wings spread _____, while a damselfly rests with its wings behind and together.

7 A dragonfly nymph lives in a _____ eating other bugs for 1-5 years.

Missing DRAGONFLY words
apart, blind, fastest, kinds, pond, wing, zoom

St. Patrick's Day: *Adjectives*

Identify these St. Patrick's Day words using your fingerspelling chart.

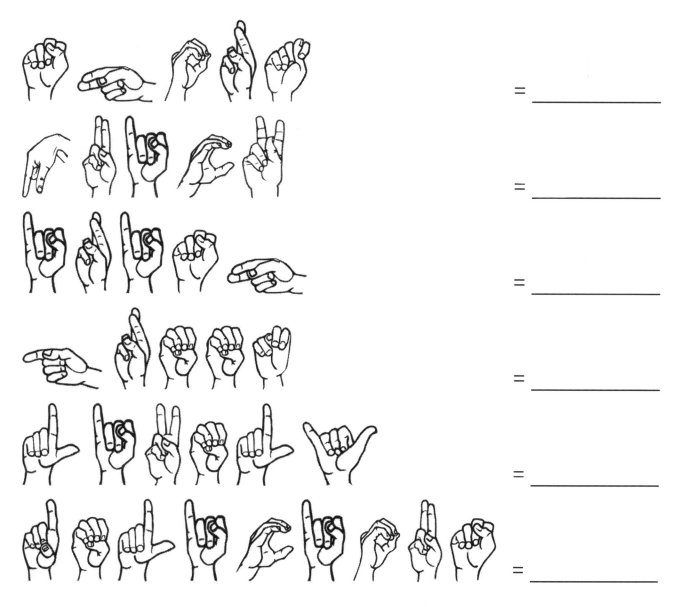

Meet the Tarantula

I see a male _____ wandering across the trail and pick it up. I'm not _____ of spiders or their enormous _____. Most _____ are, but not me. I've had them as pets, let them cling to my _____ as I walked around, let them walk across my hands, showed them to friends and laughed at their _____. Life can be scary, but I choose not to let it _____ me from doing what I want. Sometimes I put on _____. Sometimes I step back and give space, a moment, time. The rewards are cool, like this photo of a _____ when I didn't let _____ or fear stop me from experiencing life.

Missing words: afraid, fangs, fear, gloves, people, shirt, stop, tarantula, time, worry

What would a...

...mosquito say to a boy that waved it away

... light say to a moth that was flying toward it at night

... ladybug say to a roly-poly it met on a leaf

... butterfly say to a caterpillar if they met one morning

Jobs and Careers: Bus Driver

Prerequisites: What does a person have to do in order to be <u>ready</u> or <u>hirable</u> for this job?

Responsibilities: What are four things that a person does each day in this job?

number **1**

number **2**

number **3**

number **4**

Benefits: What are several benefits a person receives from doing this job?

_____

_____

_____

_____

Jobs and Careers: Carpenter

Prerequisites: What does a person have to do in order to be <u>ready</u> or <u>hirable</u> for this job?

Responsibilities: What are four things that a person does each day in this job?

1

2

3

4

Benefits: What are several benefits a person receives from doing this job?

Compare and **C**ontrast

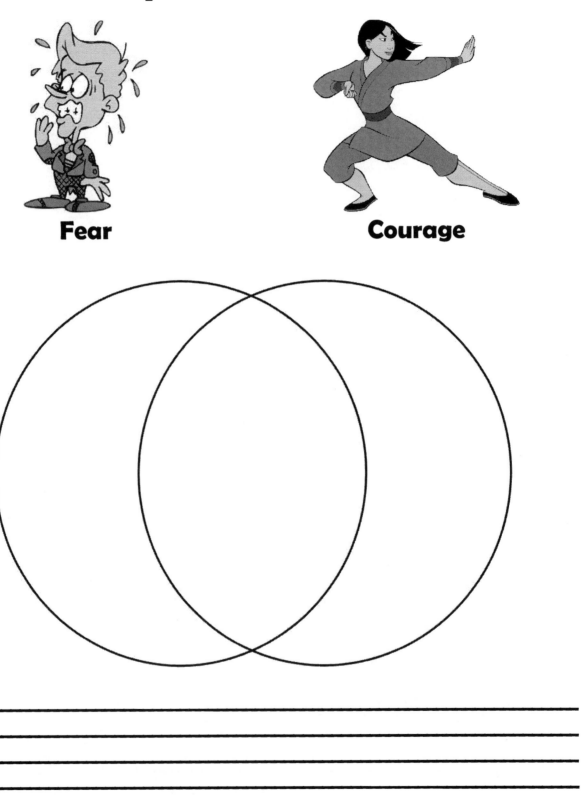

Fear

Courage

Are you afraid of strangers?

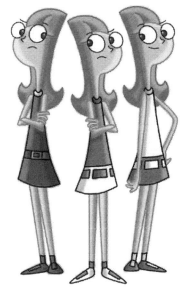 

Write a paragraph explaining how you feel when you meet someone for the first time. Are you relaxed and comfortable, or are you nervous and scared?

_____
_____
_____
_____
_____
_____
_____
_____
_____
_____
_____
_____
_____
_____
_____

Why do kids and adults play board games?

Use a <u>computer</u>, <u>tablet</u> or <u>phone</u> to search online for information about the C.I.A. and share your observations below:

1

2

3

4

5

6

Discrimination: *Unfair Wealth Distribution*

Less than one percent of Americans own eighty percent of all the wealth (land, business, stores, machines). Is that fair? Share your thoughts below:

_____

_____

_____

_____

_____

_____

_____

_____

_____

_____

_____

_____

_____

_____

_____

_____

_____

_____

$

Discrimination: *Neighbors*

Who lives nearby? Do your neighbors look like you, their skin color, their hair, their eyes? Or do they look different? Who decides if they can live nearby? Share your thoughts below:

_____

_____

_____

_____

_____

_____

_____

_____

_____

_____

_____

_____

_____

_____

Nelson Mandela

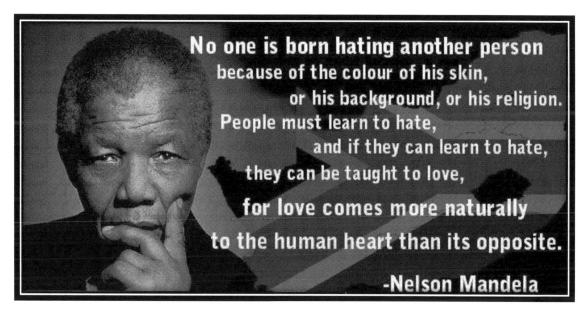

No one is born hating another person because of the colour of his skin, or his background, or his religion. People must learn to hate, and if they can learn to hate, they can be taught to love, for love comes more naturally to the human heart than its opposite.

-Nelson Mandela

Is it okay to hate someone else? Yes or no? Share your thoughts below:

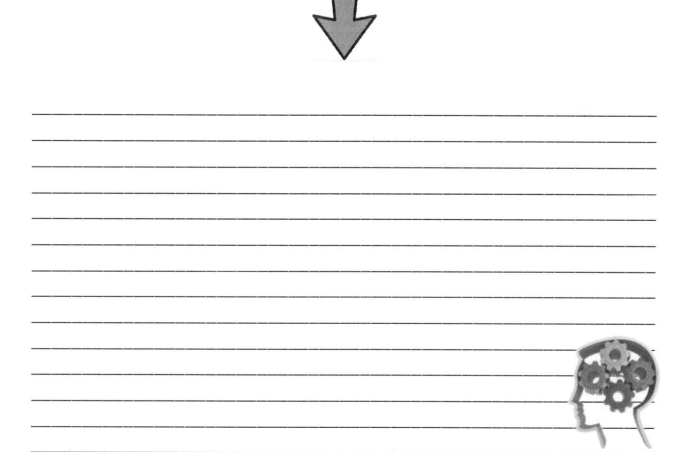

Booker T. Washington

I have learned that success is to be measured not so much by the position that one has reached in life as by the obstacles which he has overcome while trying to succeed. Out of the hard and unusual struggle through which he is compelled to pass, he gets a strength, a confidence, that one misses whose pathway is comparatively smooth by reason of birth and race.

(Booker T. Washington)

How do you become successful? What must you do? And what exactly is success? Does it have something to do with money, or owning stuff, or making things, or going places, or knowing people, or people knowing you?

Stereotypes: *Hillbillies and Rednecks*

People who grow up in the hill country are sometimes portrayed like this. What is wrong with this image? Share your thoughts below:

1

2

3

4

A to Z Word Puzzle

Use all 26 letters from A to Z to complete the words in this puzzle.

A B C D E F G H I J K L M N O P Q R S T U V W X Y Z

Analyze and Describe

Words: _____

_____

_____

Pictures: _____

_____

_____

_____

Numbers: _____

_____

Veterans Day: *Places*

Identify these Veterans Day words using your finger-spelling chart.

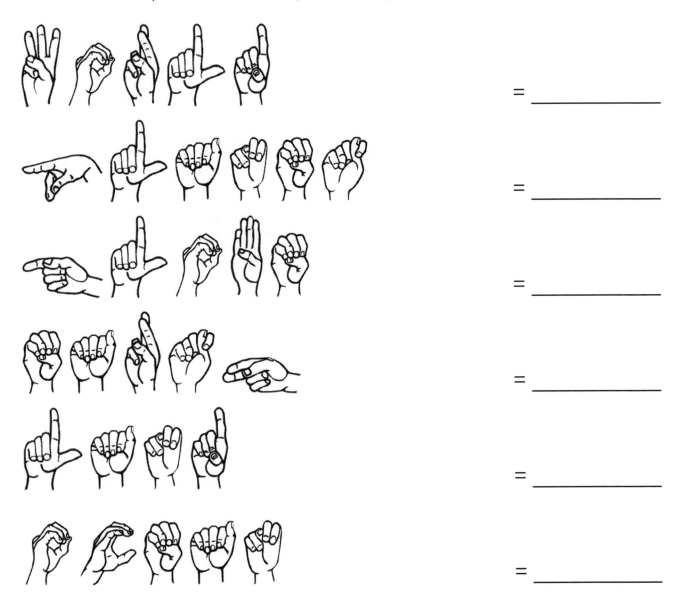

= _____

= _____

= _____

= _____

= _____

= _____

Veterans Day: *Things*

Identify these Veterans Day words using your finger-spelling chart.

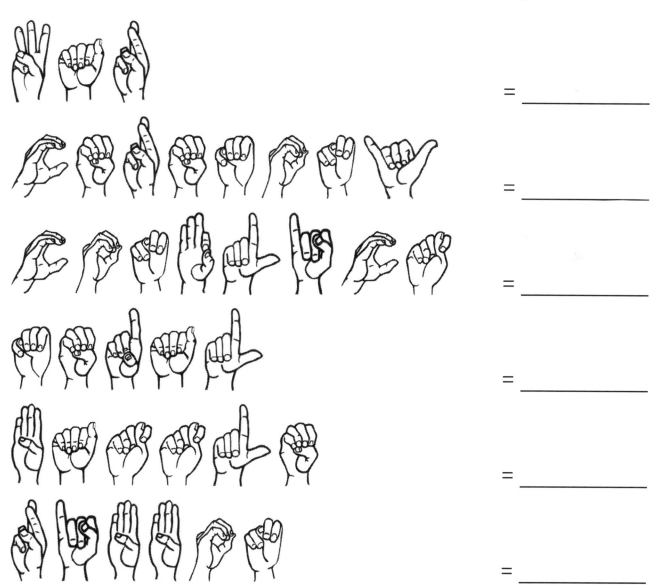

= _____

= _____

= _____

= _____

= _____

= _____

The <u>Cross</u> of Christianity

Use a phone, tablet or laptop to answer these questions.

1. Which religion uses this symbol? _____

2. What does this symbol represent? _____
_____
_____

3. In which countries is this the dominant religion? _____
_____
_____

4. When and where did this religion begin? _____
_____
_____
_____
_____

5. What are two interesting things you learned about this symbol? ___
_____
_____
_____
_____
_____
_____

SOURCE: _____
SOURCE: _____

The Star of David of Judaism

Use a phone, tablet or laptop to answer these questions.

1. Which religion uses this symbol? _____
2. What does this symbol represent? _____
_____
_____

3. In which countries is this the dominant religion? _____
_____
_____

4. When and where did this religion begin? _____
_____
_____
_____
_____

5. What are two interesting things you learned about this symbol? __
_____
_____
_____
_____
_____
_____

SOURCE: _____
SOURCE: _____

The <u>Crescent and the Star</u> of Islam

Use a phone, tablet or laptop to answer these questions.

1. Which religion uses this symbol? _____
2. What does this symbol represent? _____
_____
_____

3. In which countries is this the dominant religion? _____
_____
_____

4. When and where did this religion begin? _____
_____
_____
_____
_____

5. What are two interesting things you learned about this symbol? __
_____
_____
_____
_____
_____
_____

SOURCE: _____
SOURCE: _____

The **Wheel** of Buddhism

Use a phone, tablet or laptop to answer these questions.

1. Which religion uses this symbol? _____
2. What does this symbol represent? _____
   _____
   _____

3. In which countries is this the dominant religion? _____
   _____
   _____

4. When and where did this religion begin? _____
   _____
   _____
   _____
   _____

5. What are two interesting things you learned about this symbol? ___
   _____
   _____
   _____
   _____
   _____
   _____

SOURCE: _____
SOURCE: _____

The <u>Yin and Yang</u> of Taoism

Use a phone, tablet or laptop to answer these questions.

1. Which religion uses this symbol? _____

2. What does this symbol represent? _____
   _____
   _____

3. In which countries is this the dominant religion? _____
   _____
   _____

4. When and where did this religion begin? _____
   _____
   _____
   _____
   _____

5. What are two interesting things you learned about this symbol? ___
   _____
   _____
   _____
   _____
   _____
   _____

SOURCE: _____

SOURCE: _____

The <u>Om</u> of Hinduism

Use a phone, tablet or laptop to answer these questions.

1. Which religion uses this symbol? _____

2. What does this symbol represent? _____
_____
_____

3. In which countries is this the dominant religion? _____
_____
_____

4. When and where did this religion begin? _____
_____
_____
_____
_____

5. What are two interesting things you learned about this symbol? __
_____
_____
_____
_____
_____
_____

SOURCE: _____

SOURCE: _____

The **Khanda** of Sikhism

Use a phone, tablet or laptop to answer these questions.

1. Which religion uses this symbol? _____

2. What does this symbol represent? _____
_____

3. In which countries is this the dominant religion? _____
_____

4. When and where did this religion begin? _____
_____
_____
_____
_____

5. What are two interesting things you learned about this symbol? __
_____
_____
_____
_____
_____
_____

SOURCE: _____
SOURCE: _____

The __Pentacle__ of Paganism

Use a phone, tablet or laptop to answer these questions.

1. Which religion uses this symbol? _____

2. What does this symbol represent? _____
_____
_____

3. In which countries is this the dominant religion? _____
_____
_____

4. When and where did this religion begin? _____
_____
_____
_____
_____

5. What are two interesting things you learned about this symbol? __
_____
_____
_____
_____
_____
_____
_____

SOURCE: _____
SOURCE: _____

The **Happy Human** of Humanism

Use a phone, tablet or laptop to answer these questions.

1. Which religion uses this symbol? _____
2. What does this symbol represent? _____
_____
_____

3. In which countries is this the dominant religion? _____
_____
_____

4. When and where did this religion begin? _____
_____
_____
_____
_____
_____

5. What are two interesting things you learned about this symbol? __
_____
_____
_____
_____
_____
_____

SOURCE: _____
SOURCE: _____

How Many Triangles?

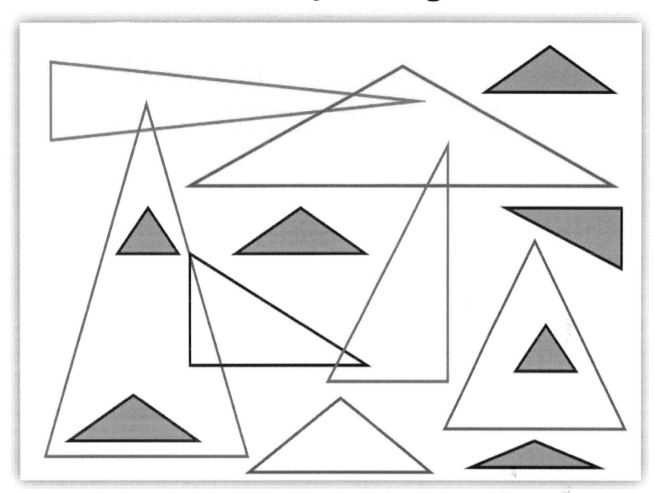

How many **shaded** triangles do you see? _____

How many triangles **overlap** another triangle? _____

How many triangles are completely **inside** another triangle?

_____

How many triangles are **alone** (NOT inside another triangle and
NOT overlapping another triangle)? _____

How many **total** triangles do you see? _____

How Many Branches?

How many <u>buttons</u> do you see? _____

How many <u>birds</u> do you see? _____

How many <u>hats</u> do you see? _____

How many <u>empty</u> things do you see? _____

How many <u>branches</u> do you see? _____

How many <u>bugs</u> do you see? _____

How many <u>eyes</u> do you see? _____

How many Mammals?

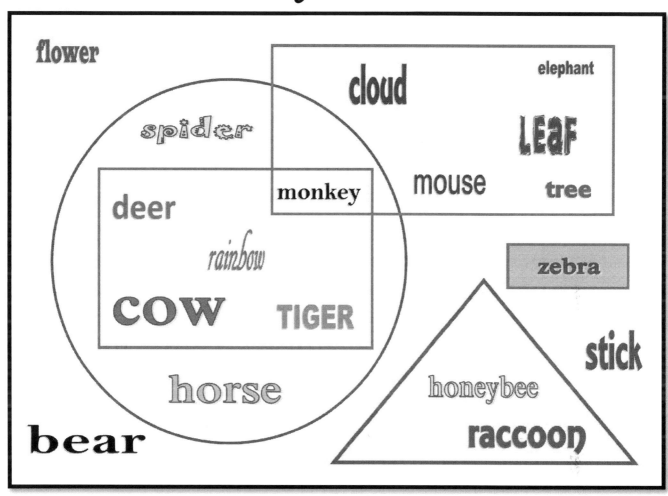

How many <u>MAMMALS</u> do you see? ____

How many <u>BUGS</u> do you see? ____

How many <u>PLANTS</u> do you see? ____

How many <u>FLIERS</u> do you see? ____

How many <u>WALKERS</u> do you see? ____

How many <u>COLORFUL</u> things do you see? ____

How many numbers?

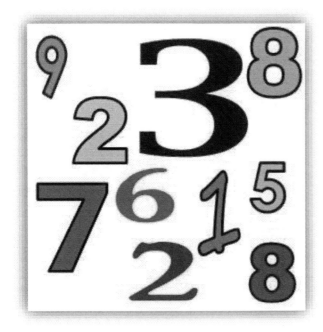 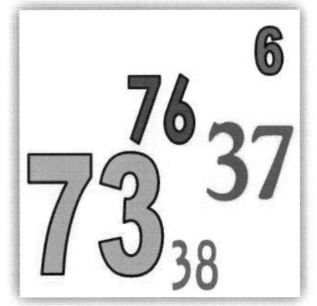

How many **one-digit numbers** do you see? _____

How many **two-digit numbers** do you see? _____

How many **even numbers** do you see? _____

How many **odd numbers** do you see? _____

How many **palindromes** do you see? _____

What is the **sum** of the two largest numbers? _____

What is the **difference** of the largest & smallest number? _____

Which number is **repeated** the most often? _____

What is Lou Gehrig's Disease?

Use a <u>computer</u>, <u>tablet</u> or <u>phone</u> to search online for answers to this question.

1 _____

2 _____

3 _____

4 _____

5 _____

ONLINE SOURCES OF INFORMATION:

_____
_____

Accomplishments of Stephen Hawking

Use a <u>computer</u>, <u>tablet</u> or <u>phone</u> to search online for information about this well-known scientist.

ONLINE SOURCES OF INFORMATION:

_____

_____

What does it take to become a scientist?

Use a <u>computer</u>, <u>tablet</u> or <u>phone</u> to search online for answers to this question.

1 ....

2 ....

3 ....

4 ....

5 ....

ONLINE SOURCES OF INFORMATION:

_____

_____

How do we learn about the universe?

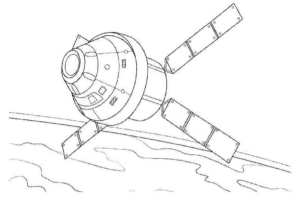

Use a <u>computer</u>, <u>tablet</u> or <u>phone</u> to search online for answers to this question.

_____

_____

_____

_____

_____

_____

_____

_____

_____

_____

_____

_____

_____

_____

_____

ONLINE SOURCES OF INFORMATION:

_____

_____

Mission San Fernando Rey de España

Use a laptop, tablet or phone to access the internet and explore this history of this mission.

<u>Who</u> founded it?

<u>What</u> is special about its name?

<u>When</u> was it founded?

<u>Where</u> is it located?

Search for two interesting facts about this mission and write them below:

SOURCES:

Mission San José

Use a laptop, tablet or phone to access the internet and explore this history of this mission.

Who **founded it?**

What **is special about its name?**

When **was it founded?**

Where **is it located?**

Search for three interesting facts about this mission and write them below:

1

2

3

SOURCES:

Things you might run away from...

Describe four <u>scary situations</u> in which you might <u>run away</u> (to keep you alive, to avoid pain or cold or discomfort, or to get away from someone who is annoying you).

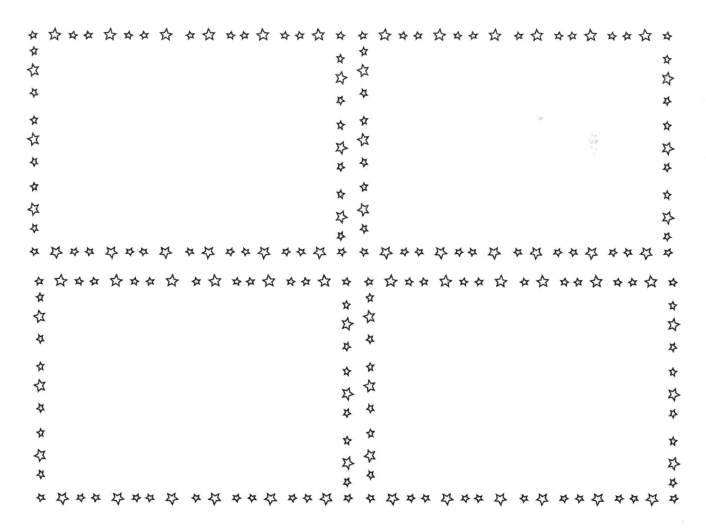

Things that make you smile...

Describe six different situations in which you might <u>smile</u>...

...on a weekend	*...at school*
...in your bedroom	*...in the dark*
...when you're wearing no shoes	*...when it is very quiet*

WEIRD STUFF TO WEAR ON YOUR HEAD...

What interesting or odd things do people wear on their <u>head</u> (other than a baseball cap)?

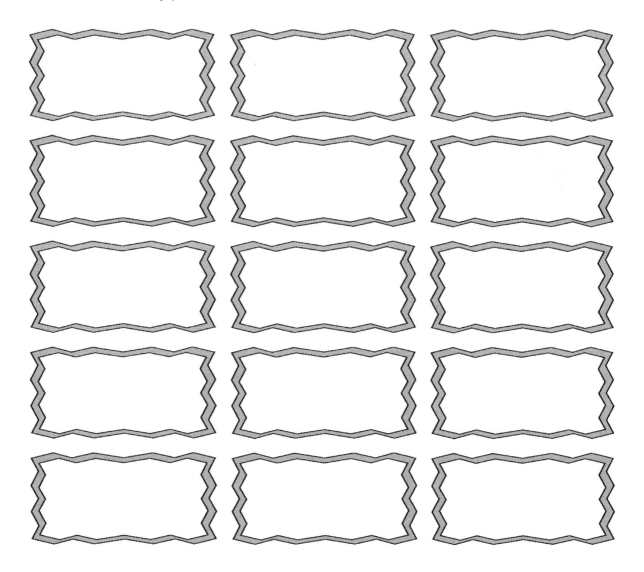

HOW TO WINK...

Describe weird stuff you can do with your <u>eyes</u> (besides looking at people or closing your eyes while you sleep).

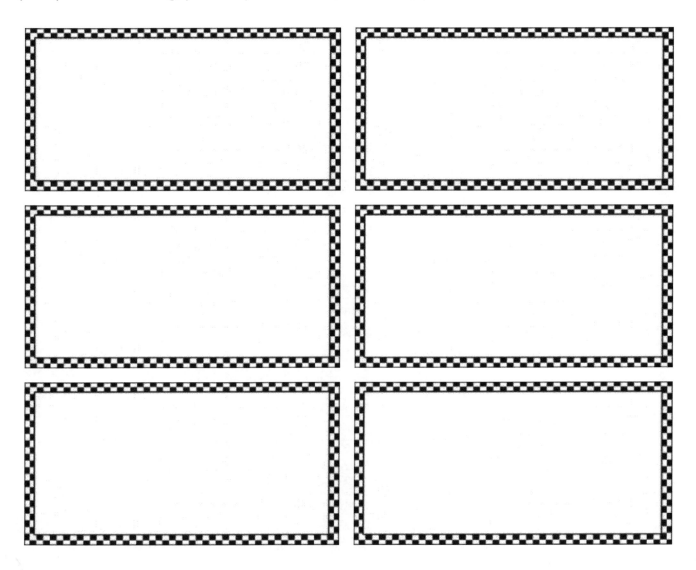

Death

In the documentary "Free Solo," we find out that many people who have climbed without ropes have fallen to their death. Is it okay for someone to take such risks with their life? Who gets to decide what is allowed and what isn't allowed? Parents? A wife or husband? Elected leaders in government? The individual climber? You may consult friends or family to stimulate your thinking. You should also use a <u>computer</u>, <u>tablet</u> or <u>phone</u> to explore what others have said about this question online. Record your thoughts below.

Okay to take risks...

↓

Not okay to take risks...

↓

_____   _____
_____   _____
_____   _____
_____   _____
_____   _____
_____   _____
_____   _____
_____   _____
_____   _____
_____   _____

Is rock climbing a safe activity?

How safe is rock-climbing (with and without ropes)? You may consult friends or family to stimulate your thinking. Use a computer, tablet or phone to explore what others have said on this topic, and record seven things you learned:

1
2
3
4
5
6
7

Airplanes

What do you know about **airplanes** and how they **fly** and what they're **made** of?

_____

_____

_____

_____

_____

_____

_____

_____

_____

_____

_____

_____

The Inca Empire

What do you know about the **Inca Empire** and what happened to them?

_____

_____

_____

_____

_____

_____

_____

_____

_____

_____

_____

_____

_____

_____

The Same or *Different*

Girl   **Boy**

What do you <u>notice</u> about these athletes from South America?

How are they the SAME?   How are they DIFFERENT?

 1   **1**

 2   **2**

 3   **3**

 4   **4**

Louisa May Alcott

Use a <u>computer</u>, <u>tablet</u> or <u>phone</u> to search online for information about this author.

1 _____

2 _____

3 _____

4 _____

5 _____

ONLINE SOURCES OF INFORMATION:

_____

_____

Jane Austen

Use a <u>computer</u>, <u>tablet</u> or <u>phone</u> to search online for information about this author.

1

2

3

4

5

6

7

ONLINE SOURCES OF INFORMATION:

_____

_____

The Hupa Tribe

What is special about this indigenous tribe of California? Go online and search for information about their <u>history</u> and <u>people</u>, their <u>religion</u> and where they <u>lived</u>, their <u>leaders</u> and the <u>language</u> they spoke.

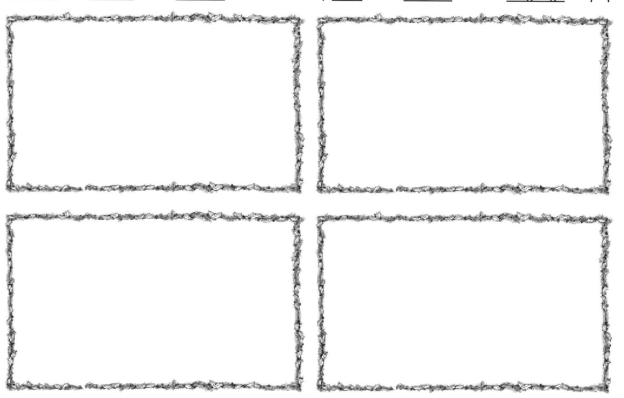

ONLINE SOURCES OF INFORMATION:

_____

_____

The Karuk Tribe

What is special about this indigenous tribe of California? Go online and search for information about their <u>history</u> and <u>people</u>, their <u>religion</u> and where they <u>lived</u>, their <u>leaders</u> and the <u>language</u> they spoke.

1

2

3

4

ONLINE SOURCES OF INFORMATION:

_____

_____

Fun with License Plates

Secret Messages

1 _____	**2** _____	**3** _____
4 _____	**5** _____	**6** _____

Which license plate was the **easiest**? _____

Which license plate was the **hardest**?

_____

Which license plate is the **funniest**? _____

Make up two new license plates with a secret message

New Plate	**Secret Message**
	= _____
	= _____

A Stamp from The Bahamas

Look closely at this stamp and describe the WORDS, NUMBERS and PICTURES that are on it.

1 _____

2 _____

3 _____

Coins from The Bahamas

Look closely at these coins and describe what you see.

①

②

③

Currency from The Bahamas

What WORDS, NUMBERS and PICTURES do you see on this bill?

 number 1

 number 2

 number 3

 number 4

 number 5

 number 6

The Same or *Different*

Puerto Rico   **The United States**

What do you <u>notice</u> about these FLAGS from The Caribbean?

How are they the SAME?   How are they DIFFERENT?

Saying Hello

Use a __computer__, __tablet__ or __phone__ to search online for information about how people greet each other using words and without using words. Write down several things that you learned:

1

2

3

4

5

ONLINE SOURCES OF INFORMATION:

_____

_____

Helen Keller

Use a <u>computer</u>, <u>tablet</u> or <u>phone</u> to search online for information about Helen Keller. Record several of the more interesting things you learned below:

_____

_____

_____

_____

_____

_____

_____

_____

_____

_____

_____

_____

ONLINE SOURCES OF INFORMATION:

⬇

_____

_____

The Eye: Different Colors

Use a __computer__, __tablet__ or __phone__ to search online for information about why humans have different colored eyes. Record information from three different websites below:

1._____
_____
_____
    SOURCE: _____

2._____
_____
_____
    SOURCE: _____

3._____
_____
_____
    SOURCE: _____

Why do we blow our nose?

Use a <u>computer</u>, <u>tablet</u> or <u>phone</u> to search online for information about why we blow our nose and what causes it to run so much in the wind, or when its cold, or when you're sick, or when you're sad...

1

2

3

4

ONLINE SOURCES OF INFORMATION:

What are boogers?

Use a <u>computer</u>, <u>tablet</u> or <u>phone</u> to search online for information about boogers. For real! What are they and why do they magically appear inside your nose? Record your findings below:

1

2

3

4

ONLINE SOURCES OF INFORMATION:

Why do farts stink?

Use a <u>computer</u>, <u>tablet</u> or <u>phone</u> to search online for information about the causes of farts. Share your observations below:

①

②

③

④

ONLINE SOURCES OF INFORMATION:

_____

_____

Sticking out your tongue

Use a <u>computer</u>, <u>tablet</u> or <u>phone</u> to search online for information about how animals use their tongue:

1

2

3

4

ONLINE SOURCES OF INFORMATION:

_____

_____

_____

What kinds of foods are poisonous?

Use a <u>computer</u>, <u>tablet</u> or <u>phone</u> to search online for information about foods that are poisonous.
Record your observations below:

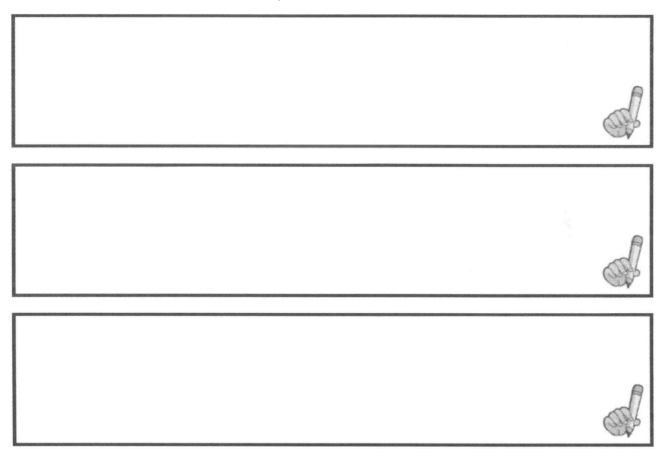

ONLINE SOURCES OF INFORMATION:

What is the purpose of your skin?

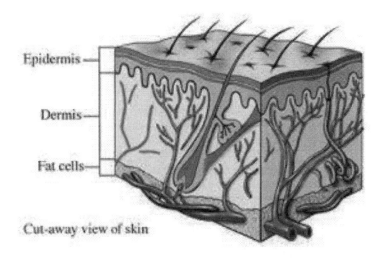

Epidermis —

Dermis —

Fat cells —

Cut-away view of skin

What does it do when it too HOT outside?

What does it do when it too COLD outside?

Why do we clean stuff?

Use a <u>computer</u>, <u>tablet</u> or <u>phone</u> to search online for information about why we use paper and chemicals to clean our hands, our face and our private parts. Record your observations below:

ONLINE SOURCES OF INFORMATION:

_____

_____

The UNITED STATES

Do you know your **states**?

This puzzle is filled with them and they can be horizontal, vertical, diagonal, forwards, or backwards.
Can you find them?

```
M A S S A C H U S E T T S C M D
K P A U L A N A I S I U O L A E
A E R T A Q S C V I D N N W R L
N N I A B I A O E L A T E E Y A
S N Z H A P X N K L H N W S L W
A S O A M P E N N I O O Y T A A
S Y N T A I T E I N D M O V N R
R L A O K S G C S O N R R I D E
B V A K E S N T N I A E K R A O
O A M A N I I I O S L V A G T D
D N O D T S M C C O S A L I O A
A I H H U S O U S I I N A N S N
R A A T C I Y T I H E A S I E A
O D L U K M W J W O D I K A N T
L K K O Y N O G E R O D A W N N
O J O S S I I A W A H N R O I O
C A L I F O R N I A R I M I M M
```

Find these states

Alabama, Alaska, Delaware, Pennsylvania, Massachusetts, Indiana, Hawaii, California, Louisiana, Arizona, Kansas, Montana, Oklahoma, South Dakota, Maryland, Minnesota, Texas, Rhode Island, West Virginia, Idaho, Iowa, Colorado, Utah, Connecticut, New York, Vermont, Oregon, Kentucky, Mississippi, Illinois, Wisconsin, Ohio, Wyoming

The greatest danger for most of us is NOT that our aim is too high, that our aim is too high, but that it is too low and we reach it.

Find these words in this Word Search below

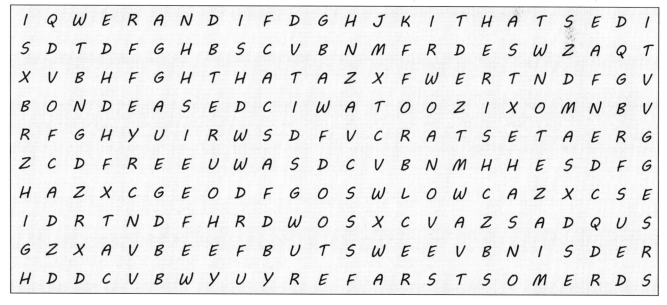

I	Q	W	E	R	A	N	D	I	F	D	G	H	J	K	I	T	H	A	T	S	E	D	I
S	D	T	D	F	G	H	B	S	C	V	B	N	M	F	R	D	E	S	W	Z	A	Q	T
X	V	B	H	F	G	H	T	H	A	T	A	Z	X	F	W	E	R	T	N	D	F	G	V
B	O	N	D	E	A	S	E	D	C	I	W	A	T	O	O	Z	I	X	O	M	N	B	V
R	F	G	H	Y	U	I	R	W	S	D	F	V	C	R	A	T	S	E	T	A	E	R	G
Z	C	D	F	R	E	E	U	W	A	S	D	C	V	B	N	M	H	H	E	S	D	F	G
H	A	Z	X	C	G	E	O	D	F	G	O	S	W	L	O	W	C	A	Z	X	C	S	E
I	D	R	T	N	D	F	H	R	D	W	O	S	X	C	V	A	Z	S	A	D	Q	U	S
G	Z	X	A	V	B	E	E	F	B	U	T	S	W	E	E	V	B	N	I	S	D	E	R
H	D	D	C	V	B	W	Y	U	Y	R	E	F	A	R	S	T	S	O	M	E	R	D	S

Other words are hidden in this puzzle that explore the quote a little more. Can you find them?

COUNTRIES OF THE WORLD

Find the hidden words. They can be horizontal, vertical, diagonal, forwards, or backwards.

```
B F R A N C E N I A P S D N A L G N E C
R E S C O T L A N D Z B A I S S U R U O
A I V I E T N A M K Q T U R K E Y B L L
Z S A U D I A R A B I A C N A P A J A O
I R A N S W I T Z E R L A N D G J T O M
L A U N I T E D B K O R E A N I H C S B
A E B I Q Z G O G H A N A D N A L E R I
Z L S V T J K C R K Q C K R A T A Q T A
T O E O S J U I T D N N O O R E M A C A
Y C T R A T R R A N Z A I R E B L R D I
N I A Y O E U O C A T J B Z R Y Q I N L
A X T J C Q G T I L G U A T E M A L A A
M E S E E K U R R I H A I T I G Z J L R
R M E L J G A E E A Q K E Z I L E B L T
E R I Q Z U Y U M H L A G U T R O P O S
G H A M A N A P A T K A I R E G I N H U
C A N A D A O F T R O D A V L A S L E A
```

Find these countries

Australia, Belize, Brazil, Cameroon, Canada, Chile, China, Colombia, Cuba, Egypt, El Salvador, England, France, Germany, Ghana, Greece, Guatemala, Haiti, Holland, Ireland, Iran, Iraq, Israel, Italy, Ivory Coast, Japan, Korea, Laos, Mexico, Nigeria, Panama, Puerto Rico, Portugal, Qatar, Russia, Saudi Arabia, Scotland, Spain, Switzerland, Thailand, Turkey, United States of America, Uruguay, Vietnam, Zaire

Our SOLAR SYSTEM

This puzzle is full of planets and moons and words that relate to our solar system. They can be horizontal, vertical, diagonal, forwards, or backwards. Find them.

```
E A R T H U I N E M E G T E N A L P V
K Y X A L A G D U O L C E L T S G R E
R I N G S K Y Y K L I M L B R T A O N
M N A T M O S P H E R E E B O R L B U
M V S C E T I L L E T A S U O O I E S
E B T H Y D R O G E N T C H T N L P O
T M E T E O R N E G Y X O Y F O E H L
S G R A V I T Y D F A T P G A M O O A
Y T O N E P T U N E W S E O R Y Z B R
S E I R C R A T E R S I E L C A X O T
Y K D U H G D L R O W T V O E N U S C
R C J T E M O C P O U N L M C A O U A
U O K A P O L L O I Y E O S A T T N P
C R L S P A C E E R T I V O P I U A M
R O R B I T R I T O N C E C S T L R I
E A W N O I R E P Y H S R E T I P U J
M O O N Q N A M U H E T I R O E T E M
```

Find these words

Sun, Mercury, Venus, Earth, Mars, Jupiter, Saturn, Uranus, Neptune, Pluto, planet, moon, orbit, solar system, revolve, gravity, space, asteroid, meteor, meteorite, comet, scientist, telescope, cosmology, astronomy, spacecraft, rocket, probe, impact, crater, world, atmosphere, Hyperion, Phobos, Titan, Triton, satellite, human, Apollo, Gemini, oxygen, hydrogen, Galileo, Hubble, rings, Oort Cloud, Milky Way Galaxy,

WHAT IS MISSING?

Something is MISSing
in this puzzle.
What?
Well, words that start with
the letters MIS-
They can be **horizontal**,
vertical, **diagonal**,
forwards, or **backwards**.
Can you find them?
I hope so.
Good luck, and don't
make too many mistakes...

```
I M I S P R O N O U N C E M M M
M I S D E M E A N O R S I I I I
I S T I M I S S P E A K S S S S
S C S M I S U S E S M S C G S H
S O U I S C I M S I M H S U M A
I N R S S O M I S M I S S I I P
M D T S I U M S I E S M I D S S
I U S S M N M M F M N S M E T I
T C I S I T I E I O S I D N E
C T M I S S M L S S M I S S I V
E I S M S I B I S S E M S S R A
R M I S L A B E L I R I S S P H
I M I S R E P R E S E N T I S E
D M S E M I S E K A T S I M I B
S I S I S S I M E R I F S I M S
I I M I M I S F O R T U N E S I
M I S A L I G N E D T I F S I M
```

Find these words that start with MIS-

misaligned, misbehave, mischief, misconduct, miscount, misdemeanor, misdirect, miserable, misfire, misfit, misfortune, misguided, mishap, mislabel, misnomer, misprint, mispronounce, misrepresent, misspeak, mistake, mistrust, misuse

Bonus: Can you find the four letter word MISS? It's there, many times. How many can you find? __

Honesty

Hey, it's about time you admit the truth. TRUTH!
It's here, on this page, over and over again.
Can you find it?
It can be **horizontal**, **vertical**, **diagonal**, **forwards**, or **backwards**.

```
T R U T H U T H T U R T H T U T
T R U R R H R T U H T U R T T R
T H U U H U U H U T T U H U T U
R T H T R U T H T U H H T U R T
U R T H H R H H T R U T H T U H
T U U H U T T R U T H U T U T H
H T T T H U T T U H U R H T T H
T H H U R U H T T R U T H U T T
T R U T H H T U H T U R T U T R
U T R U T H R H U H T H R H H U
T H T U H T R U T H U T T U T T
T R U T H U T H R T U U H T U H
R T U U T R H U U R H R U T R H
U R H T T T H T T U T T R U T H
T U T R U T H T H T U T U H U T
H T U R H T R U T H H T U R T H
T U T R U T H T T U H T U R T U
```

Is It okay to lie?

_____

_____

_____

_____

_____

What Do You Know about Money?

Is anything really free ?

Where does money come from ?

Why do we use money ?

How much money do you have right now ?

FREE

Is paper money better than metal money ?

What happens if you take something without paying for it ?

Have you ever used a credit card at a store ?

Why do people use banks ?

_____

_____

_____

_____

_____

_____

_____

_____

_____

_____

_____

_____

What Do You Know about Pizza?

What does pizza look like ?

What is your favorite topping on a pizza?

Have you ever eaten an entire pizza ?

Do you like cold pizza ?

When is pizza an excellent meal option ?

What is the most important rule about pizza ?

Do you like to dip your pizza in Ranch Dressing ?

What drink do you like with pizza ?

_____

_____

_____

_____

_____

_____

_____

_____

_____

_____

_____

Matching Compound Words

Connect two words with a line to form a compound word.

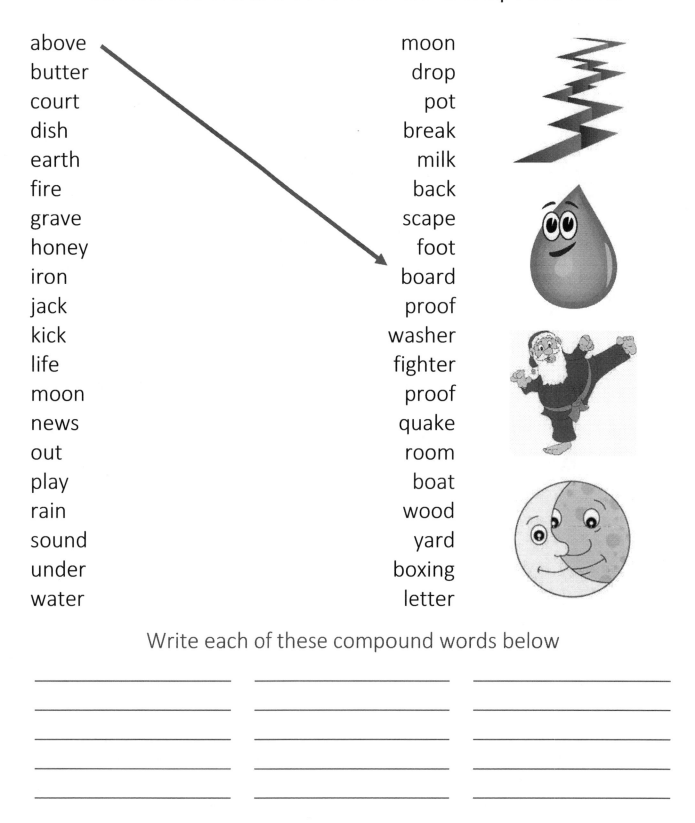

above	moon
butter	drop
court	pot
dish	break
earth	milk
fire	back
grave	scape
honey	foot
iron	board
jack	proof
kick	washer
life	fighter
moon	proof
news	quake
out	room
play	boat
rain	wood
sound	yard
under	boxing
water	letter

Write each of these compound words below

_____   _____   _____

_____   _____   _____

_____   _____   _____

_____   _____   _____

_____   _____   _____

Matching Compound Words

Connect two words with a line to form a compound word.

air   cake

black   worm

cheese   line

door   jack

earth   stop

fire   mother

grand   some

horse   proof

irk   knife

jack   hair

knap   shoot

life   sack

moon   sprint

new   line

off   shine

pepper   fall

rain   ware

spring   mint

table   case

upper   time

Write each of these compound words below

_____ _____ _____

_____ _____ _____

_____ _____ _____

_____ _____ _____

_____ _____ _____

Analyze and Describe

The Eisenhower Dollar

(1971 to 1978)

Describe six interesting things that you see on the **front** and **back** of this dollar coin.

WORDS
⬇

PICTURES
⬇

NUMBERS
⬇

Analyze and Describe

Presidential Dollar: Abraham Lincoln
(2010)

Describe six interesting things that you see on this dollar coin.

fact 1

fact 2

fact 3

fact 4

fact 5

fact 6

COMPARE and CONTRAST

Sacagawea Dollar

Peace Dollar

What is the SAME and DIFFERENT about the <u>front</u> of these Dollar coins?

How are they the same?   How are they different?

_____

_____

_____

_____

_____

_____

_____

_____

_____

_____

_____

_____

_____

_____

_____

_____

_____

_____

_____

_____

What does it mean to be bi-sexual?

Internet Safety

1

Do your work. Don't play around. You have an assignment to do, so focus your attention where it is supposed to be.

2

Search for answers to the questions. Don't get caught going down rabbit holes in search of weird or strange stuff.

3

Imagine that your mother is sitting on your right and your teacher is sitting on your left, watching what you're doing. What would they say to you right now? Make good choices.

Answers

A to Z Word Puzzle #3 (Answers)

Use all 26 letters from A to Z to complete the words in this puzzle.

	K		F		T		C
H	I	D	B	O	T	H	E	R
	T	I	G	E	R	I		I
A	T	E		G	I	R	L	S
	E		C	E	N	D		P
E	N	J	O	Y	D		B	Y
Q		M	A	Z	E		E	
U	N	D	E	R	X		G	
A		O	D		W	A	S	
L	E	G	S	E	V	E	N	

A B C D E F G H I J K L M N O P Q R S T U V W X Y Z

A to Z Word Puzzle #4 (Answers)

Use all 26 letters from A to Z to complete the words in this puzzle.

		L		A		S	U	C	H
J	A	I	L		Q	O	
E		Z			U	O	U	
E	X	A	M	P	L	E	P	
P		R		A	O	
	D	W	E	L	L	I	N	G
	H	V	H	
E	N	T	R	Y	O	
R	E	S	
B	R	E	A	K	F	A	S	T

A B C D E F G H I J K L M N O P Q R S T U V W X Y Z

Geometric Activities

Fourteen circles; I'm the man (or, "I'm da man"), me first

Twenty-nine circles; I get A's; too cute to be true

Hidden Nouns

SPACE: planet, moon, asteroid, comet, star, orbit, gas, galaxy, universe, Mercury, Venus, Earth, Mars, Milky Way

SUMMER: sun, vacation, ball, toy, pool, lake, ocean, beach, game, book, movie, park, playground, heat, shade

Multiplication: What Is Missing?

1 largest odd two-digit: 45
2 smallest even two-digit: 12
3 multiples of six: 12, 18, 30, 36, 48
4 even: 2, 4, 8, 12, 14, 18, 20, 28, 30, 32, 36, 40, 48, 50, 56, 70, 80

Fingerspelling: Veterans Day

Persons: soldier, private, general, sergeant, warrior, fighter;

Places: world, planet, globe, earth, land, ocean;

Things: war, ceremony, conflict, medal, battle, ribbon;

License Plates

1-Don't Test Me, 2-I Mountain Bike, 3-It's Too Quiet, 4- Little Wimp, 5- On Accident, 6-Plllleeeeeease,

1-Generator, 2-House Cleaner, 3-[See You] Later Alligator, 4-On Purpose, 5-Pie Maker, 6-Too Goofy,

Compound Words

aboveboard buttermilk courtroom dishwasher earthquake firefighter graveyard honeymoon ironwood jackpot kickboxing lifeboat moonscape newsletter outbreak playback raindrop soundproof underfoot waterproof

airline blackjack cheesecake doorstop earthworm fireproof grandmother horsehair irksome jackknife knapsack lifeline moonshine newsprint offshoot peppermint rainfall springtime tableware uppercase

If you would like more enrichment for your students, I have hundreds of workbooks for educators available at Amazon.com. Just search for "C. Mahoney" and any of these subject areas: Math, Writing Prompts, Gifted & Talented, Back to School, Summer, Word Puzzles, Wildlife, Journals, Activity books, Sign Language, Frequently Misspelled Words, Brainteasers, or Spelling. For example...

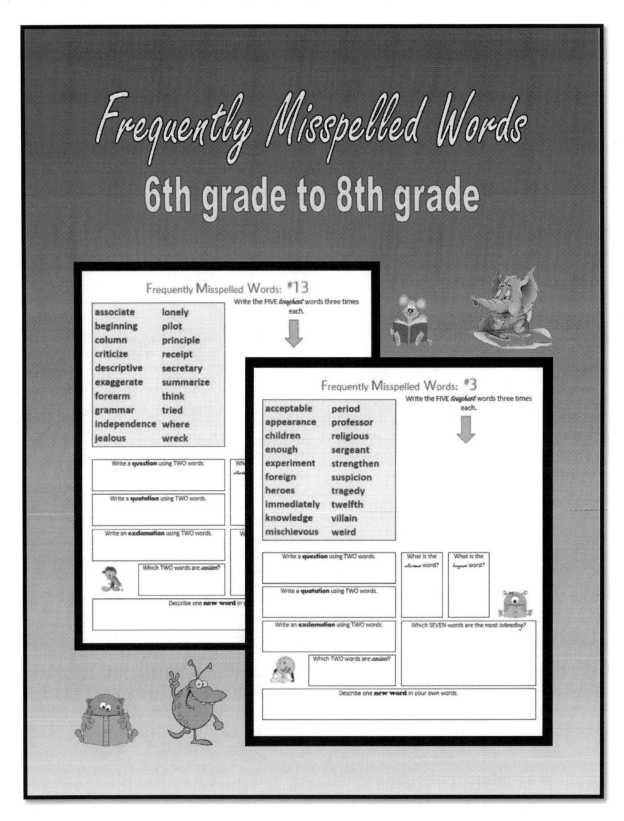

Made in the USA
San Bernardino,
CA